RODOLPHE KREUTZER

Forty-Two Studies for the Viola

Transcribed for the Viola and edited by
WALTER BLUMENAU

Published in 2022 by Allegro Editions

ISBN: 978-1-63561-981-2 (casebound)
978-1-63561-982-9 (paperback)

ALLEGRO EDITIONS

Forty-Two Studies

R. Kreutzer
Transcribed for viola and edited by
Walter Blumenau

- u = upper part of bow
- l = lower part of bow
- WB. = whole bow
- A = A-string
- D = D-string
- G = G-string
- C = C-string
- I = first position
- II = second position
- etc.
- ——— (Dash) = leave the finger on the string to the end of the dash
- ⌐ = put down the finger in preparation for a note to come

1

Adagio sostenuto

Forty varied bowings for the performance of Study No. 2

4

Twenty-nine varied bowings for the performance of Study No. 5

6

7

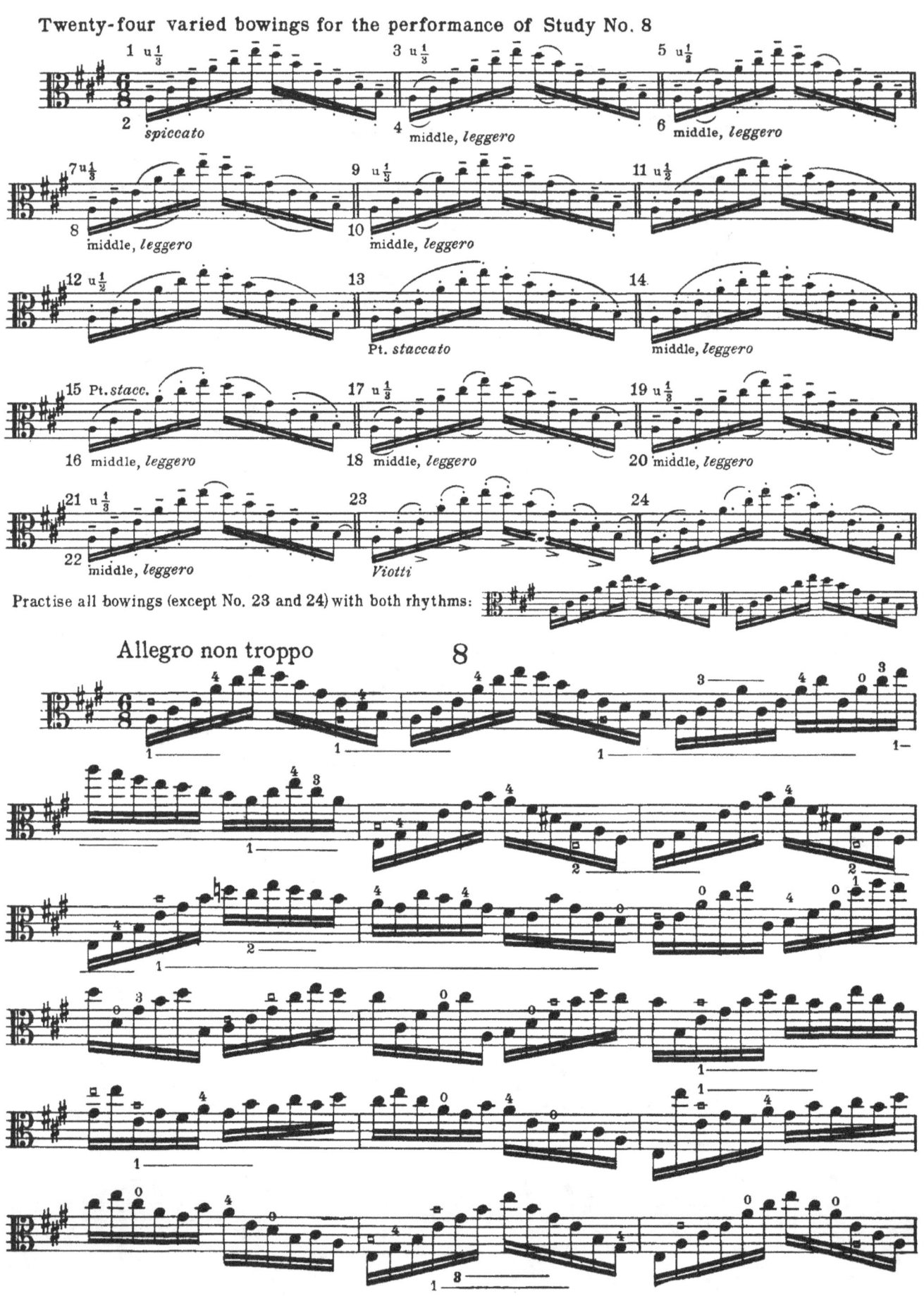

9

Allegro moderato

10

11

12

21

16

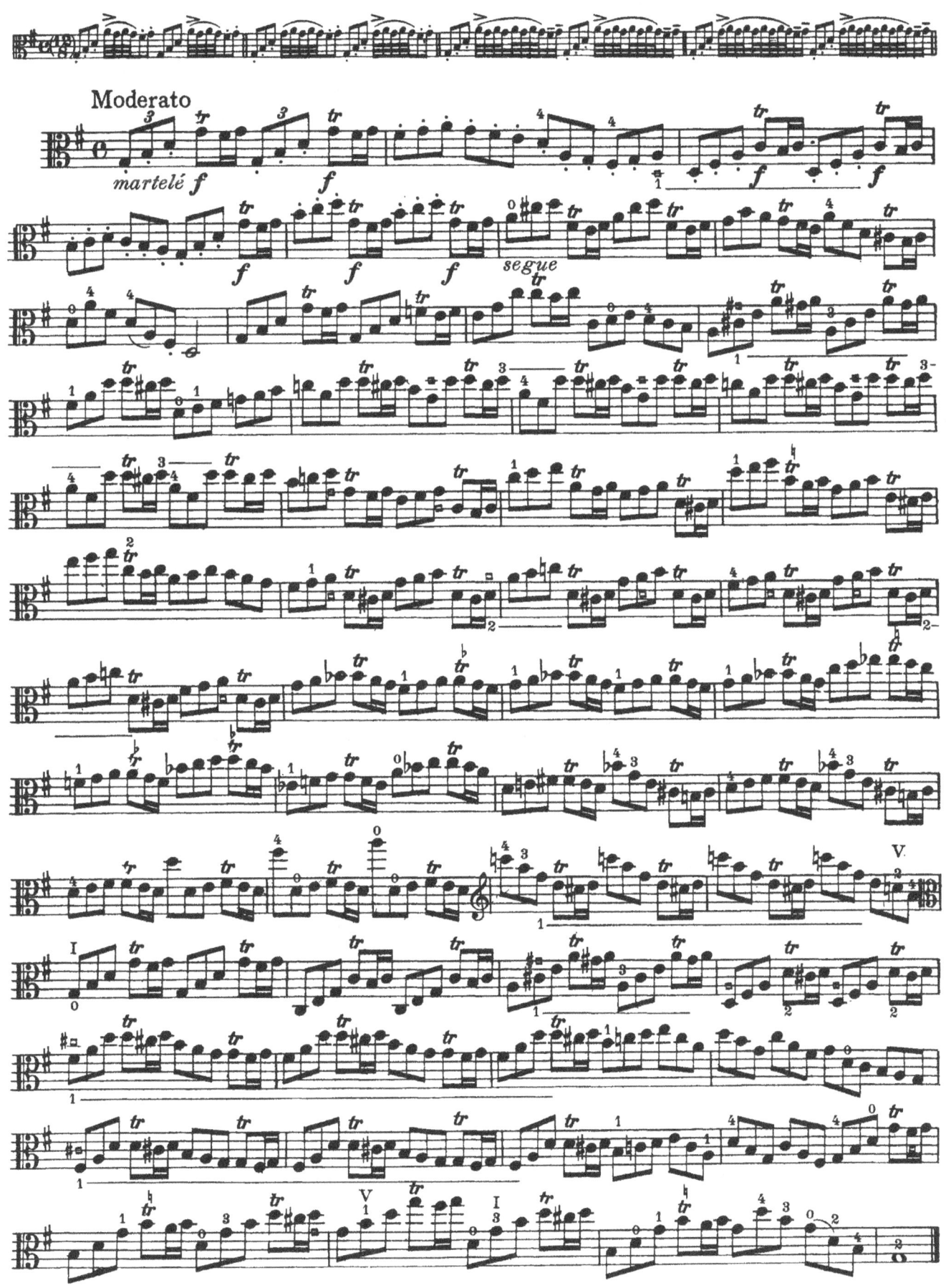

Editors differ in their rhythmical analyses of the first quarter beat. It is given here in accordance with the notation presented in authentic old editions, and should be practised in that way. The two following variants are also recommended:

*In some editions this rhythm is given:

18

27

19

22

33

23

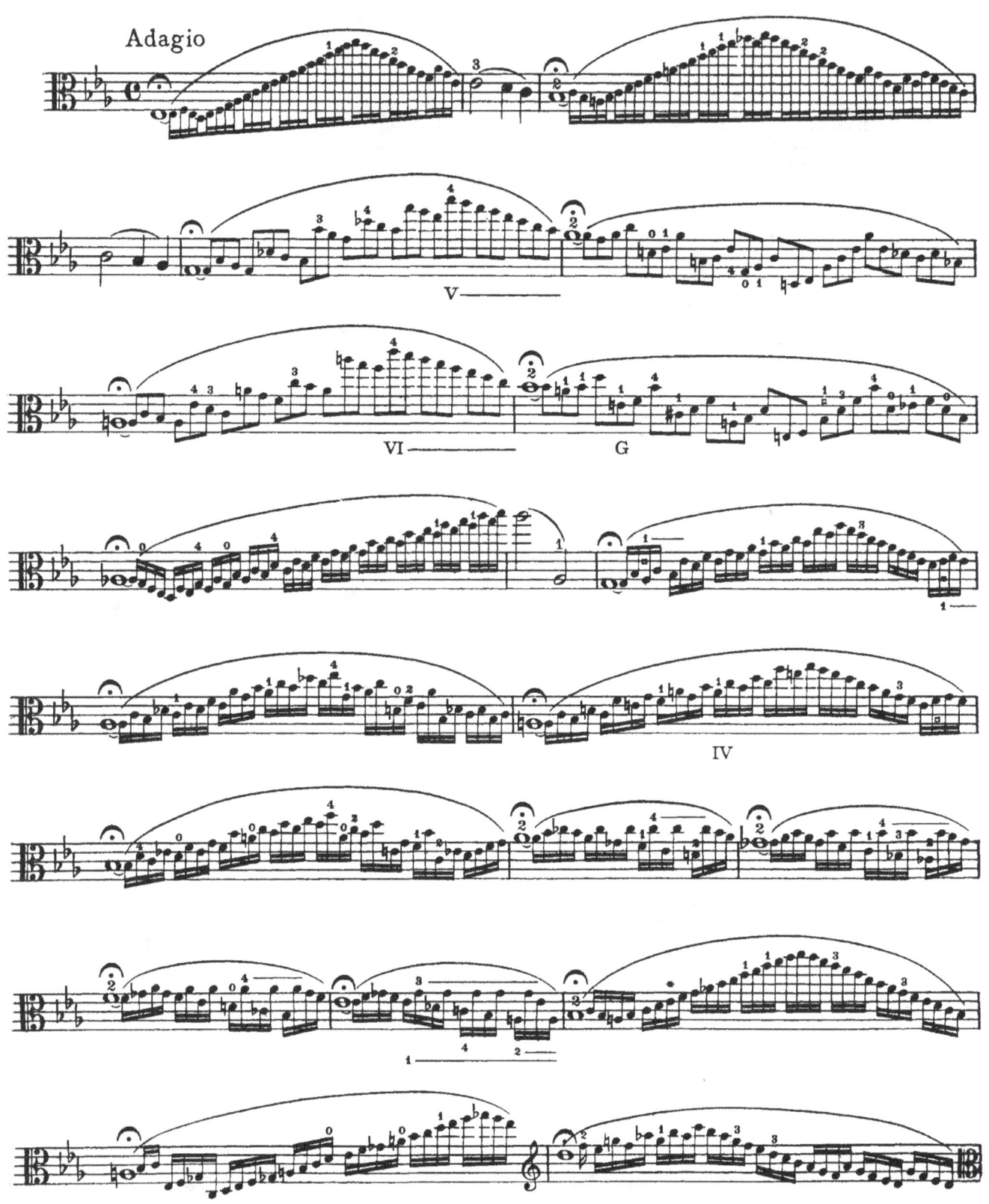

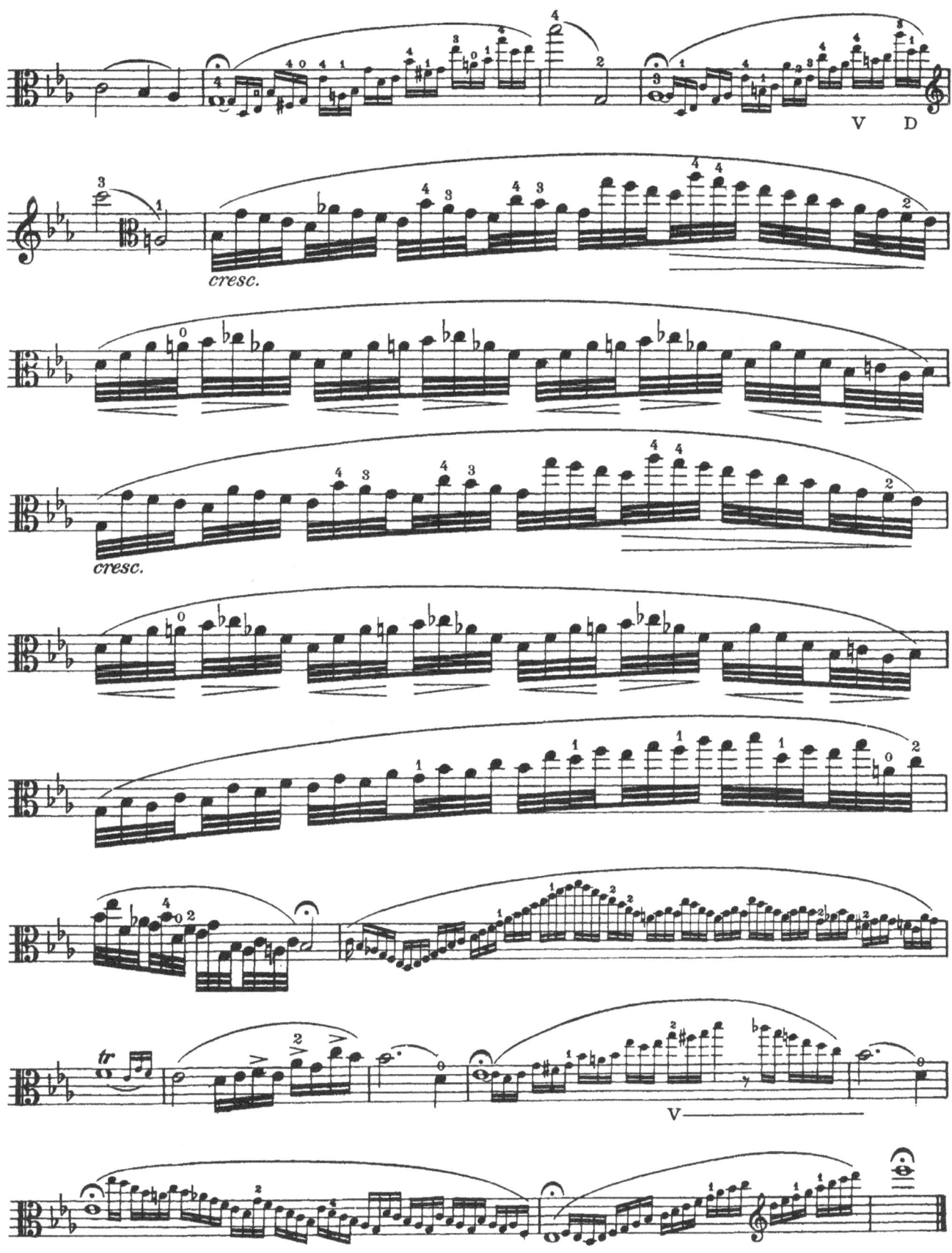

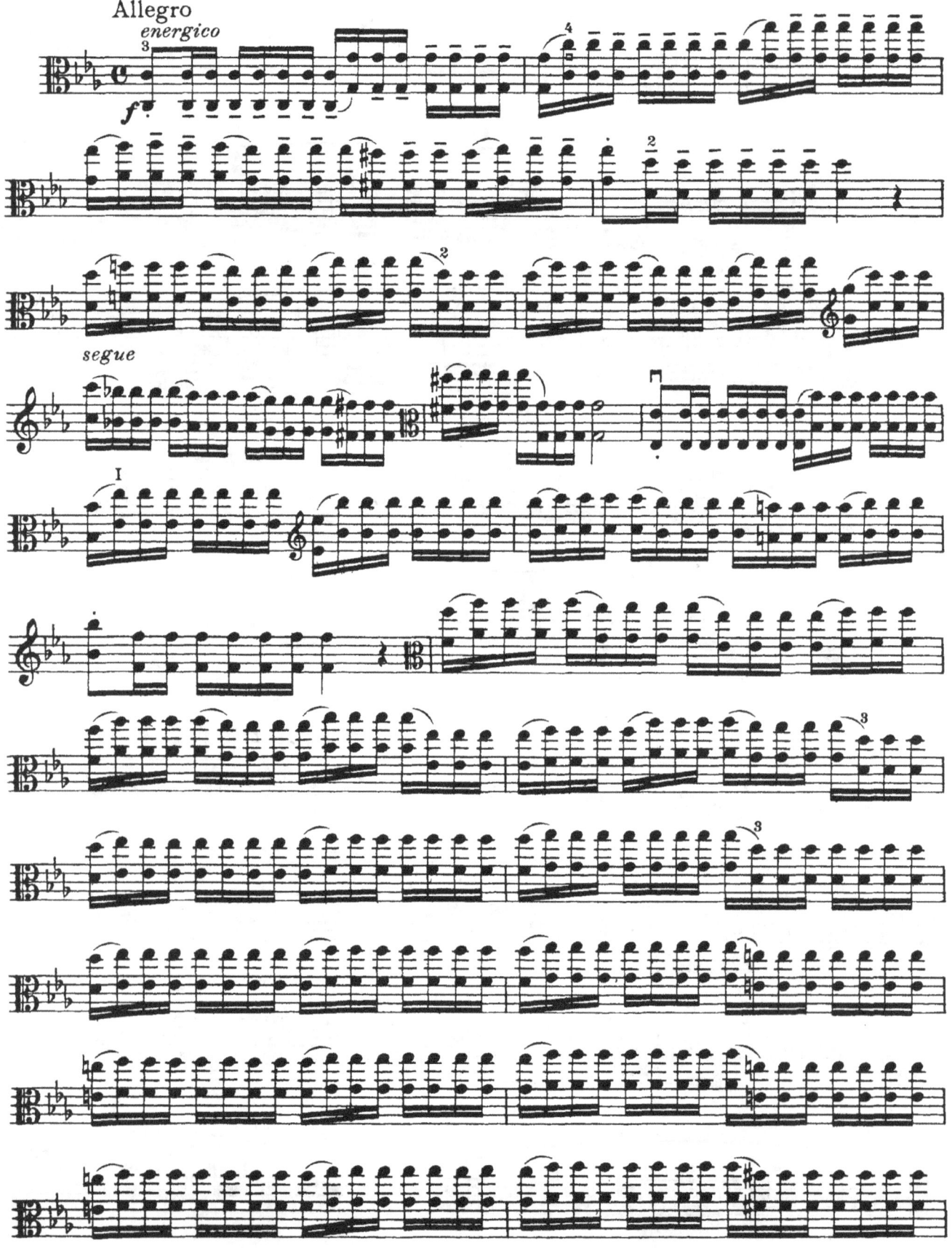

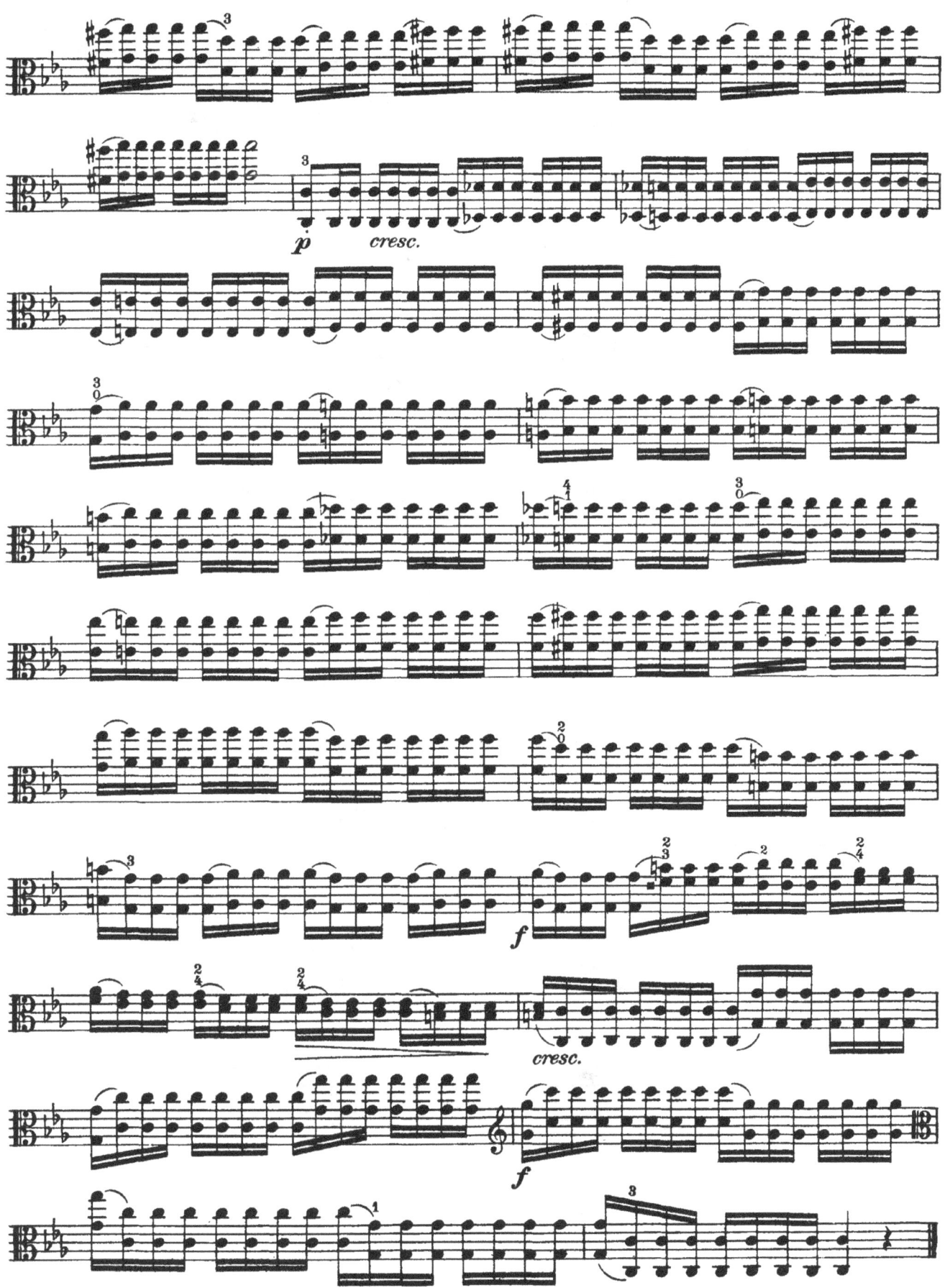

25

26

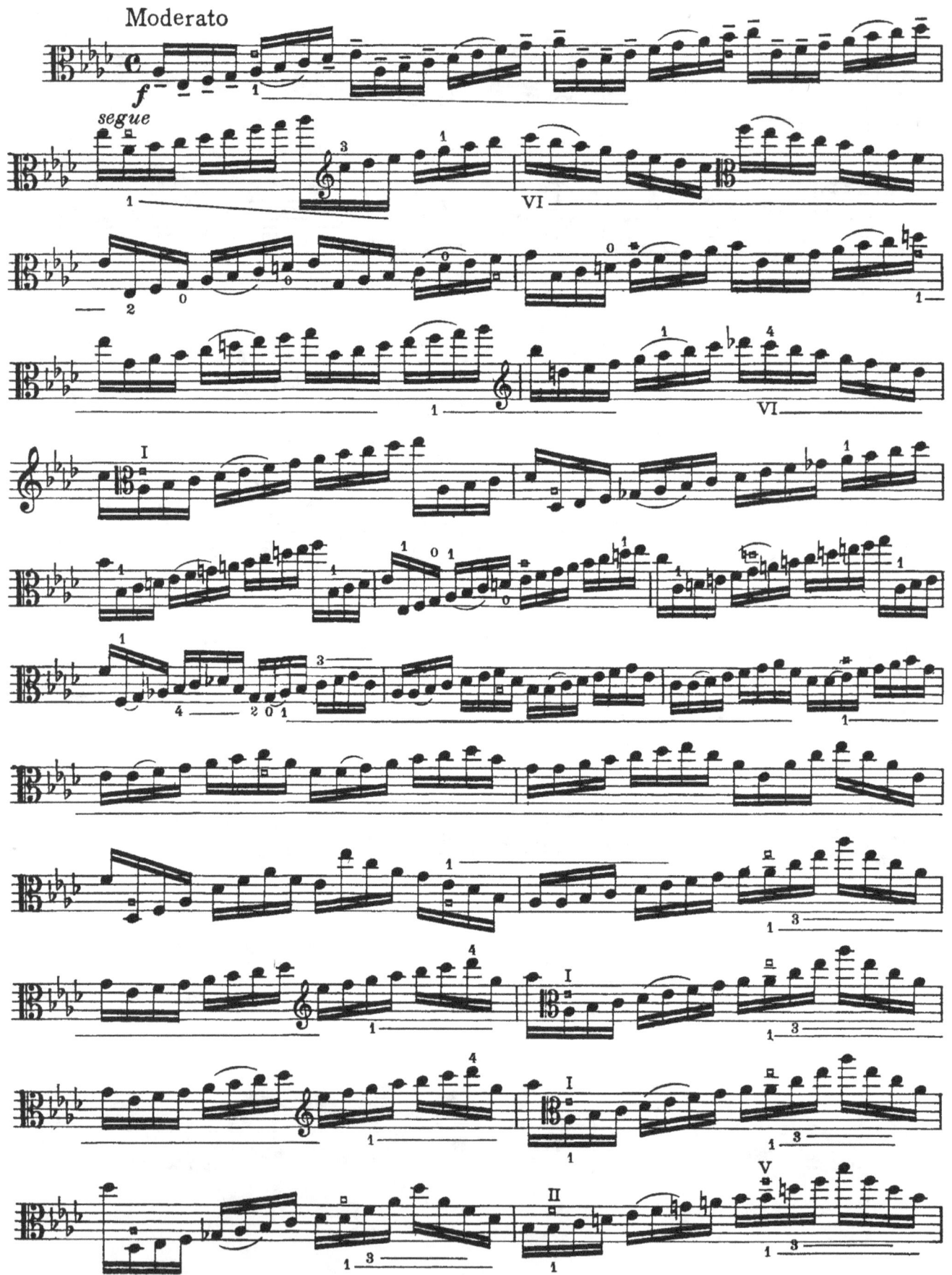

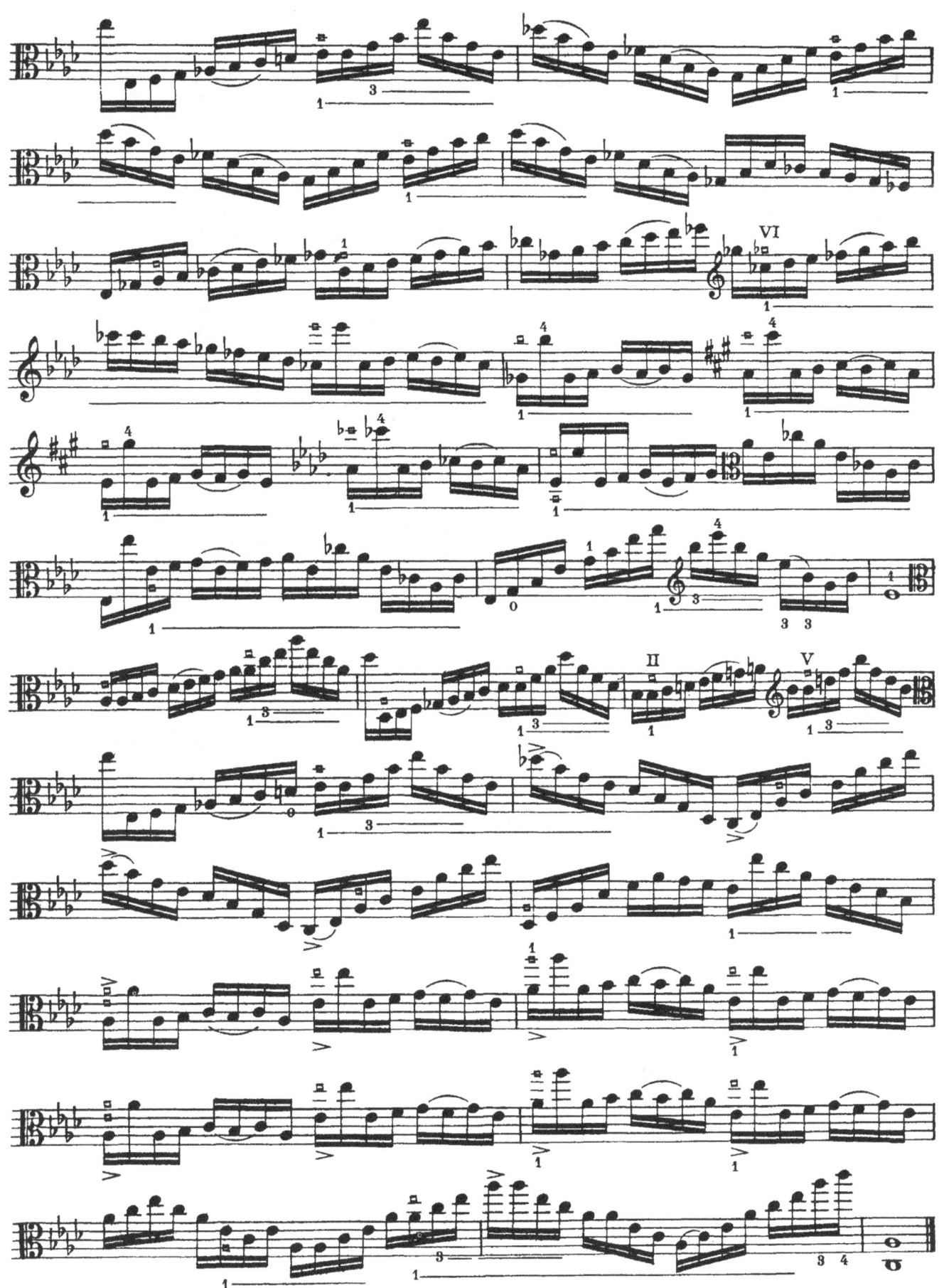

27

43

28

a) Firm staccato at the point.

29

Moderato, tranquillo

30

31

51

32

33

34

55

35

March
Allegro maestoso

36

59

37

38

40

Grace note indicates starting trill with upper note.

41

www.ingramcontent.com/pod-product-compliance
Lightning Source LLC
Chambersburg PA
CBHW081328040426

42453CB00013B/2336